Healthy Behaviors

BY MEGAN BAILEY

The Child's World

Published by The Child's World®
1980 Lookout Drive • Mankato, MN 56003-1705
800-599-READ • www.childsworld.com

Acknowledgments
The Child's World®: Mary Berendes, Publishing Director
Red Line Editorial: Editorial direction
The Design Lab: Design
Amnet: Production
Photographs ©: Front cover: Comstock; Shutterstock/hartphotography;
Shutterstock/Tom Burlison; Shutterstock/Meelena; Shutterstock/Arvind
Balaraman; PhotoDisc; Shutterstock/Arvind Balaraman, 3; BrandX,
4, 6, 15, 19; Shutterstock/Fotokostic, 5; FoodIcons, 6; Shutterstock/
hartphotography, 7, 21; Shutterstock/Anna Omelchenko, 9;
Comstock, 10, 13, 14, 17, 21; Shutterstock/Leah-Anne Thompson, 11;
Shutterstock/serrnovik, 16; Shutterstock/Meelena, 21; PhotoDisc, 21

ISBN: 978-1623235369
LCCN: 2013931383

Printed in the United States of America
Mankato, MN
July, 2013
PA02174

ABOUT THE AUTHOR

Megan Bailey is a freelance writer who works from her home in Chicago. She loves kids, pets, especially cats, and the Chicago Cubs.

Table of Contents

CHAPTER 1   Healthy Choices   4

CHAPTER 2   Healthy Communication   10

CHAPTER 3   Healthy You   14

Hands-on Activity: Healthy Choices
*   Art Project*   20
Glossary   22
To Learn More   23
Index   24

CHAPTER ONE

Healthy Choices

Parker and Max always sit together for lunch. One day, Parker watched Max pull a bag of potato chips, two cupcakes, and a can of soda from his lunch box. Puzzled, Parker looked down at his own lunch. He had a turkey sandwich topped with lettuce and tomato, some carrot sticks, a carton of milk, and a cup of yogurt for dessert. Where were Max's vegetables and fruits? Where were his sandwich and carton of milk? Didn't he know that eating healthy foods helps create a healthy you?

The boys went to recess after lunch. Max ran out to join a group of kids playing soccer, but Parker sat down on a bench to watch his classmates

play basketball. Max wondered why Parker usually sat through recess. Didn't he know moving around every day helps you stay healthy and fit?

Max ran up to Parker as they came in from recess. Max invited Parker to play soccer at recess the next day. He wanted to show him how fun it is to be active. Parker also had something to share. He told Max that eating more fruits, vegetables, and **protein** would give him more energy for soccer than cupcakes and potato chips do.

Before sitting down at his desk, Parker promised Max that he would try soccer at recess the next day if Max brought carrot sticks and a turkey sandwich for lunch. Max thought that was a great idea. The next day, Max brought healthy foods with him for lunch, and Parker played soccer at recess. They both felt better after making healthy choices.

▼ *Finish a meal of beef kabobs with some juicy blueberries.*

Making good choices, such as eating a healthy diet and moving around, gives you more energy and makes you feel better about yourself. Kids need a balanced diet filled with fruits, vegetables, grains, protein, and dairy. These foods give you the energy and **nutrients** you need for a strong body and mind. Kids also need to be active for at least 60 minutes every day to stay healthy. Team sports, dancing, karate, and even doing chores around the house can help you stay active.

▶ *Getting enough sleep helps you do better in school.*

Another healthy decision is choosing to get enough sleep every night. Kids need between 8 1/2 and 12 hours of sleep each night to be ready for school and to avoid illness. The body uses sleep to grow and function properly. If you do not get enough sleep, you may feel groggy at school, and you may be sluggish on the baseball field. Getting 8 1/2 to 12 hours of sleep every night will help your brain develop and your body grow.

Making healthy choices has another important positive effect. Healthy decisions can raise your **self-esteem**. Self-esteem is the way you view and value yourself. Having good self-esteem can help you make healthy choices in your life. Knowing what you are good at and what makes you special is what gives you a good self-image. Taking care of yourself by making healthy decisions can also make you feel good about yourself.

BUILDING SELF-ESTEEM
There are many ways to build healthy self-esteem. Finding things you are good at, like dancing or sports, can help you feel good about yourself. Not sure what you are good at? Learning new things is one of the best parts about finding what makes you special. Try out for a new sport or learn how to play a musical instrument. Find something that interests you, and you are bound to have fun learning!

▶ *Opposite page: Making healthy choices, like picking good friends, helps build self-esteem.*

CHAPTER TWO

Healthy Communication

Making healthy choices is only one type of healthy behavior. Practicing good **communication** can help you deal with hard situations and build good listening skills. Healthy communication is an important tool to deal with difficult things, such as **stress**.

People feel stress when they are upset or nervous about something. Having friends and family to communicate with is a healthy way to deal with stress. One of the first steps to healthy communication is talking. When you are feeling stressed, talking to a friend, a family member, or a

▶ *Opposite page: Don't let stress overwhelm you. Talk with a friend, teacher, or parent to feel better.*

▼ *Learning to communicate well helps reduce stress.*

teacher is a healthy way to deal with your feelings. Just talking about how you feel can sometimes help make the stress go away. Also, your friend or family member will probably have some good advice to help you deal with what is making you feel stressed.

Another important step in healthy communication is being an active listener. **Active listening** involves making eye contact with the person who is speaking to you and listening to what he or she says without getting distracted or interrupting him or her. A good tip for being an active listener is to turn off the TV, the computer, or anything else that may distract you when someone is talking to you. Choosing healthy communication by talking about your feelings and being an active listener is a great way to deal with stress. It also helps you be a better friend.

FEELING STRESSED? EAT AN ORANGE!
Talking to an adult is often the best way to reduce stress. However, changing how you eat may help you feel better, too. A handful of pistachio nuts or almonds or a few slices of an orange can reduce the effects of stress on your body. Next time you are feeling stressed, try munching on these stress-busting snacks!

A good way to help keep stress away is to give yourself a **balanced life** by making sure you have enough time for school, sleep, and play. When you have less stress in your life, you can be a more positive person with a healthier self-image.

▶ *Being an active listener helps you build stronger friendships.*

CHAPTER THREE

Healthy You

▶ **Opposite page: Unhealthy peer pressure and bullying can make you feel bad about yourself.**

▼ **Sometimes, peer pressure from friends can help you make good decisions.**

Making healthy choices and learning how to communicate well will help you stay happy and healthy. However, sometimes other people will try to put you down or make you feel bad about yourself. When these times come, you need the right tools to handle them in a healthy way.

Peer pressure is when other people your age try to get you to make choices or act in a certain way. Peer pressure can be a good thing. Friends can teach us a lot of good things, like how to

play sports or how to play a musical instrument. In chapter one, Parker and Max used peer pressure in a positive way to help each other make healthy decisions. When you have friends who also make

◄ *Choosing healthy behaviors helps you and your friends stay happy and healthy.*

▼ *Friends can help you make good decisions.*

healthy choices, they can influence you to be a good decision maker, too.

However, peer pressure can happen in other ways. It can be easy to spot when someone is telling you to do something. Peer pressure can also happen when someone's bad choices influence others to make unhealthy choices. If someone has a friend who smokes or uses drugs, he or she may begin to think **substance abuse** is a good idea, too. Substance abuse is the use of drugs or alcohol. Substance abuse is very dangerous. It is also very unhealthy, since it can change the way your brain works and can make you sick.

Peer pressure can sometimes lead to an unhealthy behavior called **bullying**. Bullying is when a person or group of people tries to make someone feel bad about himself or herself.

Bullying can be done with words, such as with name-calling or other insults. Other times bullying means physically trying to harm someone.

Kids can do several things to avoid unhealthy peer pressure. Saying no or walking away from someone who is pressuring you can be difficult. However, once you try it, you will build confidence and self-esteem. Confidence and self-esteem will make it easier to walk away and say no to peer pressure in the future.

Sometimes, saying no to peer pressure is easier when you have support. Find friends who make healthy choices and help you make healthier decisions, too. With friends like these, it is easier to say no to others who pressure you to make unhealthy choices. When you feel overwhelmed by

BULLYING AT SCHOOL
Bullying has become a serious issue in schools. When a kid regularly experiences it, bullying can cause other problems in his or her life. Bullying can make kids feel sad and nervous. Kids who are bullied will often find it hard to do well in school. The best way to handle bullying is to talk to an adult you trust, like a parent or a teacher.

peer pressure, it is always a good idea to talk to an adult. Adults can help you feel better and can give you tips on how to say no to peer pressure in the future.

▶ *Good friends can help you say no to unhealthy choices.*

Hands-on Activity: Healthy Choices Art Project

The healthy choices art project is a fun way to express yourself and to show the differences healthy choices can make in your life!

What You'll Need:

Construction paper or poster board, markers, crayons, or paint

Directions:

1. First, draw or paint a scene that shows you making healthy choices and how they make you feel. For example, you can paint a picture of your friends and you playing a favorite sport or draw a picture of you doing a favorite activity with your family. Be creative and paint what makes you happy!

2. Next, paint a picture of a scene where someone is making choices that are not healthy, such as smoking or lying. Paint how that person may feel when he or she is making bad choices.

Share your art project with your classmates or family and discuss why you think healthy choices are so important.

HEALTHY CHOICES

Glossary

active listening (AK-tiv LIS-en-ing): Active listening means making eye contact with the person who is speaking to you and listening to what he or she says without getting distracted or interrupting him or her. Active listening helps you be a better friend.

balanced life (BAL-ensed lyef): A balanced life is a life where you have enough time for school, sleep, and play. A balanced life helps reduce stress.

bullying (BUHL-ee-ing): Bullying happens when a person or group of people tries to make someone feel bad about himself or herself. Bullying can be done with words or by physically trying to harm someone.

communication (kuh-MYOO-ni-KAY-shun): Communication is exchanging information with someone. Having a conversation, sending an e-mail, or texting someone are all examples of communication.

nutrients (NOO-tree-ents): Nutrients are substances the body needs to grow. Vitamins and minerals are nutrients.

peer pressure (peer PRESH-ur): Peer pressure is when other people your age try to get you to make choices or act in a certain way. Peer pressure can cause you to make good decisions and poor decisions.

protein (PRO-teen): Protein is a part of food that provides energy for your body and contains building blocks used by the whole body. Protein is found in meat, nuts, and seeds.

self-esteem (self e-STEEM): Self-esteem is having respect for yourself and your skills. Eating a healthy diet and knowing what makes you special help build self-esteem.

stress (stress): Stress is what someone feels when they are upset or nervous about something. Problems with friends or family can cause stress.

substance abuse (SUB-stens uh-BYOOS): Substance abuse is the illegal use of drugs or alcohol. Substance abuse can cause health problems.

To Learn More

BOOKS

Auer, Jim. *Standing Up to Peer Pressure: A Guide to Being True to You*. St. Meinrad, IN: Abbey Press, 2003.

Espeland, Pamela and Elizabeth Verdick. *Doing and Being Your Best: The Boundaries and Expectations Assets*. Minneapolis, MN: Free Spirit Publishing Inc., 2005.

WEB SITES

Visit our Web site for links about healthy behaviors: **childsworld.com/links**

Note to Parents, Teachers, and Librarians: We routinely verify our Web links to make sure they are safe and active sites. So encourage your readers to check them out!

Index

active listening, 12, 22
activities,
   chores, 7
   dancing, 7, 8
   karate, 7
   team sports, 4–6, 7, 8, 16

balanced diet, 7
balanced life, 13, 22
bullying, 14, 17, 18, 22

communication, 10–13, 14, 22

healthy choices art
   project, 20

nutrients, 7, 22

peer pressure, 14–19, 22
protein, 6, 7, 22

self-esteem, 8, 18, 22
sleep, 7, 8, 13, 22
stress, 10–13, 22
substance abuse, 17, 22